UTAH

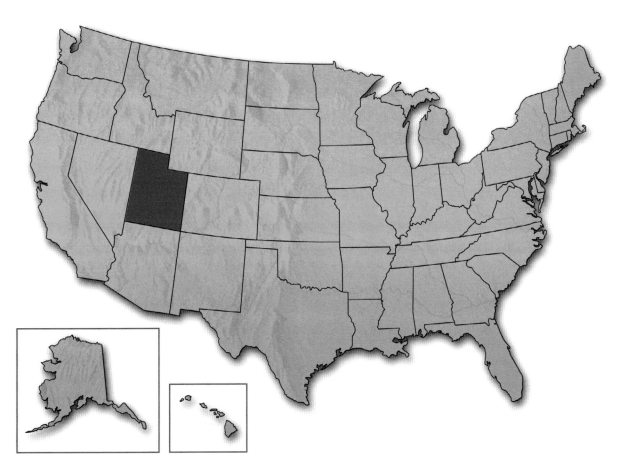

Janice Parker

Published by Weigl Publishers Inc.
123 South Broad Street, Box 227
Mankato, MN   56002
USA
Web site: http://www.weigl.com
Copyright © 2002 WEIGL PUBLISHERS INC.

Library of Congress Cataloging-in-Publication Data

Parker, Janice.
    Utah / Janice Parker.
        p. cm. -- (A kid's guide to American states)
    Includes index.
    ISBN 1-930954-18-2 (lib. bdg.)
     1. Utah--Juvenile literature. [1. Utah] I. Title. II. Series.

F826.3 .P37 2001

200126002

    ISBN 1-930954-61-1 (pbk.)

Printed in the United States of America
1 2 3 4 5 6 7 8 9 10   05 04 03 02 01

Project Coordinator
Jennifer Nault
Substantive Editor
Rennay Craats
Copy Editor
Heather Kissock
Designers
Warren Clark
Terry Paulhus
Photo Researcher
Angela Lowen

Photograph Credits
Every reasonable effort has been made to trace ownership and to obtain permission to reprint copyright material. The publishers would be pleased to have any errors or omissions brought to their attention so that they may be corrected in subsequent printings.

Cover: Angel Arch (Steve Mulligan Photography), Honeycomb (Corel Corporation); **Church of Jesus Christ of Latter Day Saints:** pages 22BR, 23BL, 24T; **Corbis Corporation:** pages 6T, 13BR; **Corel Corporation:** pages 9T, 11B, 11ML, 14T, 14BR, 14BL, 29B; **Defense Visual Information Center:** page 13T; **Steve Mulligan Photography:** pages 3T, 4T, 4BR, 8T, 8B, 9BR, 10T, 10BR, 12T, 20BL; **Photodisc Corporation:** pages 15T, 15B, 22BL; **Photofest:** pages 3B, 24ML, 24BR, 25BL, 26T; **Salt Lake Convention and Visitor's Bureau:** pages 5T, 20T, 26BL, 27B; **Sundance Film Festival:** page 7BL; **USDA:** page 9ML; **Utah Division of Indian Affairs:** page 23BR; **Utah House of Representatives:** page 21B; **Utah State Historical Society:** pages 16T, 16B, 17T, 17BL, 18T, 18B, 19T, 19M, 19B; **Utah Travel Council:** pages 3M, 4ML, 5BL, 6B, 7T, 7BR, 10ML, 11T, 12B, 13BL, 17BR, 20BR, 21T, 22, 23T, 25T, 25BR, 26BR, 27T, 28T, 28B, 29T.

CONTENTS

Arches National Park in Utah has about 1,000 arches. It is the world's most concentrated collection of these unusual rock formations.

INTRODUCTION

Utah is located in the mountain region of west-central United States. The state's unique terrain includes snowcapped mountains, sparkling lakes, deep valleys, barren salt flats, and remote deserts. Utah also has a rugged plateau region, which features strange rock formations and rainbow-colored canyons.

Utah's varied landscape makes it a great place for recreational activities. The state is home to five national parks, two national recreational areas, several national monuments, and forty-five state parks. Many Utahns enjoy activities such as boating, swimming, fishing, hiking, and skiing.

The Colorado River, which flows through southeastern Utah, is used for irrigation, hydroelectric power, and recreation.

QUICK FACTS

In 1933, the blue spruce was chosen as the official state tree. The blue spruce grows at high elevations in the Wasatch and Uinta Mountains.

Utah entered the Union on January 4, 1896 as the forty-fifth state.

The state nickname is "The Beehive State." This name comes from the state's original name, *Deseret,* meaning "land of the honeybee." The beehive is a symbol of Utahns' hard work and industry.

Salt Lake City International Airport serves over 20 million passengers every year.

Getting There

Utah lies in the western portion of the United States mainland, about halfway between Canada and Mexico. Its neighbors include Colorado to the east, Wyoming to the northeast, and New Mexico, which lies in the southeast. Nevada lies to the west, Idaho is to the north, and Arizona is to the south. Utah has one international airport—the Salt Lake City International Airport. There are about 120 airports, most of which are private, that serve the state. Visitors to Utah can take advantage of the bus services that connect Utah's main cities. The state also offers road travelers more than 40,500 miles of public highways.

QUICK FACTS

The state flag consists of a shield on a blue background. The shield is made up of the motto emblem and symbols, including a lily for peace and an eagle for protection. The flag was adopted in 1913.

The state capital is Salt Lake City.

The state motto is "Industry."

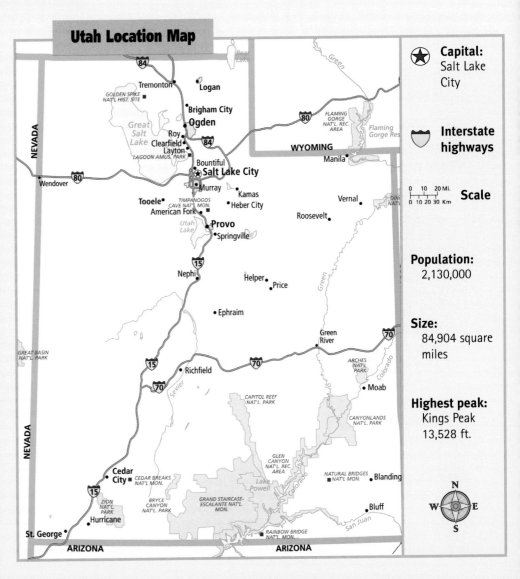

Utah Location Map

Capital: Salt Lake City

Interstate highways

Scale

0 10 20 Mi.
0 10 20 30 Km

Population: 2,130,000

Size: 84,904 square miles

Highest peak: Kings Peak 13,528 ft.

Many people flock to Utah to enjoy its beautiful scenery.

Visitors to Utah will be amazed by the state's wealth of cultural and historical spots. At This is the Place State Park, people can experience a historic village that re-creates life in a typical mid-1800s Utah community. This park **commemorates** the many people who have called Utah home over the years. Early residents of present-day Utah include Native Americans, Spanish explorers, Mormon pioneers, and mountain men.

Utah offers an array of cultural sites and activities, including museums, festivals, and theater houses. The state boasts more than 150 museums and attractions that feature a wide range of subjects. There are art galleries, national parks, and historic sites. The state also has many science-based attractions, such as botanical gardens and zoos.

Old Deseret Village, at This is the Place State Park, is an early pioneer town complete with houses, schools, churches, and shops.

QUICK FACTS

Many people believe that the town Levan, which is "navel" spelled backwards, was so named because it is at the center, or navel, of the state.

Every year in July, Wellsville hosts the Festival of the American West. There, people can dress up as cowboys and mountain men and listen to cowboy poetry and country music.

The name "Utah" comes from the Ute tribe. *Ute* means "higher" or "people of the mountains."

Salt Lake City was originally named Great Salt Lake City. "Great" was dropped from the name in 1868.

Lake Utah has 1,960 miles of shoreline, more than the entire west coast of the United States.

Early Mormon settlers dealt with low rainfall in the region by building **irrigation** systems. Many Mormons worked hard and became very successful at farming the land. They built settlements and grew prosperous. Today, the total area of farmland in Utah is relatively small, yet it is productive. Hay, corn, barley, and wheat are the state's main crops, but livestock and livestock products earn Utah farmers the most money.

In Utah's early years, mining and farming were key economic activities in the region—and this is still the case. In more recent years, manufacturing and tourism have grown considerably in the state. With Utah's many national parks, monuments, ski resorts, and the annual Sundance Film Festival, the state has become a popular destination for tourists.

QUICK FACTS

The state song, "Utah, We Love Thee," was first sung by 1,000 children on January 6, 1896. It was adopted as the state song on February 10, 1917.

Utah is the driest state after Nevada.

The Sundance Film Festival is held in Park City every year. This festival, which features independent films, is held for ten days in late January.

Newspaper Rock has petroglyphs that are about 2,000 years old. They were carved by local Native Peoples. Most of the carvings are of animals, hunters, and horsemen.

LAND AND CLIMATE

The state of Utah obtains a large amount of water from the Colorado River and its tributaries.

Utah is made up of three land regions: the Middle Rocky Mountains, the Basin and Range Province, and the Colorado Plateau. The Rocky Mountains form the northeastern part of Utah. Uinta and Wasatch are the major **mountain ranges** in this area. The western third of the state is part of the Great Basin, called the Basin and Range Province. This area contains Utah's Great Salt Lake Desert. The Colorado Plateau, in the southeastern part of Utah, covers about half of the state. The Colorado River winds through this region, flowing by colorful canyons, arches, and natural bridges.

Utah's climate differs from region to region. Most of the state enjoys hot, dry summers and mild winters. Still, the mountain regions are usually much cooler. The average July temperature in Utah ranges from less than 60° Fahrenheit in the mountain regions to more than 80°F in the southern part of the state. January temperatures drop to 35°F in the south and a chilly 20°F in the mountains.

QUICK FACTS

The Great Salt Lake Desert receives less than 5 inches of **precipitation** per year. The mountain areas, on the other hand, can receive about 50 inches of precipitation each year.

The Uinta Mountain Range is the only major range in the United States that runs in an east–west direction.

The Great Salt Lake is so salty that people can easily float in it. The lake is the saltiest in North America. Worldwide, only the Dead Sea is saltier.

The Four Corners is the meeting point of four states: Colorado, New Mexico, Arizona, and Utah. These states all meet at right angles.

Wind erosion has created many beautiful and unusual rock formations in the dry, high desert of southeastern Utah.

Dry farming, a farming method that requires very little water, was invented in Utah.

NATURAL RESOURCES

Utah is rich in mineral deposits. The state is a leading producer of copper, most of which is mined in Bingham Canyon. Gold and silver are also mined in Utah. In fact, Utah is the nation's third-largest gold producer. Iron and uranium are also mined in the southern part of the state. Utah is the only state that produces Gilsonite, which is used in road oil and asphalt tile. Gilsonite has been produced in Utah since the 1880s. Natural gas, petroleum, and coal are other resources found in the Colorado Plateau. These resources make up about two-fifths of Utah's mining revenue. Salt and other minerals are obtained from the Great Salt Lake. Clay, limestone, and gravel are also important to the state.

Soil is another valuable natural resource in Utah. The soil supports many crops, such as hay, wheat, and barley. In addition, much of the land is suitable for grazing livestock.

QUICK FACTS

Copper, which is a good conductor of heat and electricity, was first discovered in Utah in the 1860s.

Bingham Canyon has one of the largest open-pit mines in the world.

Magnesium, cement, fluorite, potash, and mercury are all found in Utah.

More than one-quarter of Utah is forested.

More than 10 percent of the copper mined in the United States comes from the Bingham Canyon Copper Mine in Utah.

PLANTS AND ANIMALS

Dinosaurs once roamed the region of present-day Utah. **Allosaurs** lived there more than 140 million years ago. This meat-eater was about 16.5 feet tall, 39 feet long, and weighed about 4 tons. Other dinosaurs, including the **stegosaur**, also lived in the area. Dinosaur National Monument in northeastern Utah is the site of many dinosaur **fossil** discoveries. Large dinosaur tracks have also been found in the southern part of the state.

There are many forests in Utah. Trees common to the area include firs, pines, poplars, and willows, as well as the state tree, the blue spruce. Cacti grow in the desert areas. Wildflowers, including the yucca and the Indian paintbrush, prosper throughout the state.

In desert regions, flowering plants bloom during the spring and summer. At higher elevations in the mountains, strong winds and a short growing season prevent trees from growing to full height. At the highest elevations, only grasses, mosses, and **annuals** grow.

QUICK FACTS

The official state flower, the sego lily, was adopted in 1911. Early Mormon settlers ate the bulbs of the sego lily during their first winter, when food was scarce.

Sagebrush is the most common shrub in Utah.

The Rocky Mountain elk became the official state animal of Utah in 1971. Elk live throughout Utah and are especially plentiful in mountain areas.

The allosaur is the state fossil.

Fossils of the Camarasaurus, a plant-eating dinosaur, can be found in Utah, Colorado, Wyoming, and New Mexico.

Many large mammals call Utah home. American black bears, mule deer, mountain lions, elk, and pronghorn antelope live in various parts of the state. Porcupines and raccoons are common sights in the mountain regions. Some desert animals remain in their dens or **burrows** during the middle of the day when temperatures are at their highest. Utah's desert animals include wild horses, coyotes, Gila monsters, rattlesnakes, and kangaroo rats.

Bird-watchers can spot great horned owls, roadrunners, hummingbirds, and red-tailed hawks in the desert. The state is also home to numerous game birds, including the ring-necked pheasant, ruffed grouse, and Gambel quail.

There are many eagles and hawks in the state. Hawkwatch International, an organization created to protect **birds of prey** and their environment, has its headquarters in Salt Lake City. Several animals native to Utah are **endangered**, including the black-footed ferret, bald eagle, gray wolf, and desert tortoise.

QUICK FACTS

The Gila monster, which is the only poisonous lizard in the United States, can be found in the southwest corner of Utah.

A fifth-grade class lobbied to make the honeybee the state insect in 1983.

Utah's state fish is the rainbow trout.

Many birds, such as the Canada goose, mallard, and the canvasback, pass through Utah as they migrate.

Utah's state bird is the California gull, a type of sea gull.

TOURISM

With five national parks and forty-five state parks, visitors have many opportunities to enjoy the outdoors.

Tourism is a major industry in Utah. People come from all over the world to experience the state's historic sites and natural areas. Summer is the most popular tourist season. Travelers can explore the many parks and historic sites in the state. Brave tourists can also tackle Utah's gushing waters by river rafting. In the winter, visitors ski and snowboard at Utah's many ski resorts.

Visitors to Dinosaur National Monument can watch **paleontologists** digging for dinosaur bones. They can also learn how fossils are cleaned and preserved. Tourists who visit Arches National Park can ramble around more than 2,000 natural stone arches.

Salt Lake City is a popular tourist destination. Temple Square is the most visited site in the state. Brigham Young, an important Mormon leader, selected this location for the temple in 1847.

Brigham City is another tourist attraction in Utah. It is home to the Golden Spike National Monument, which marks the 1869 completion of the first **transcontinental** railroad in the world.

Quick Facts

The tourism industry employs more Utahns than any other industry.

More than 18 million tourists travel to Utah each year.

Utah has fourteen mountain ski resorts. The state has billed itself as home to the "Greatest Snow on Earth." Some ski areas receive 500 inches of dry powder annually, which is excellent for skiing.

About 3 million skiers visit Utah every year.

The Mormon temple in Salt Lake City took forty years to build.

The 2002 Olympic Games in Salt Lake City are a large tourist attraction.

The Golden Spike Re-enactment re-creates the driving of the last spike in the first transcontinental railroad.

F-16 Fighting Falcons and C-130 Hercules aircraft are maintained at Hill Air Force Base in Utah.

INDUSTRY

There are many different industries in Utah that contribute to the economy of the state. Traditionally, agriculture and mining were important industries. Today, the manufacturing, transportation, finance, and service industries, including tourism, employ the largest number of people in the state.

Nearly one-third of Utahns work in the service industry. Service industry jobs include waiting on tables in restaurants and repairing computers. About 22 percent of Utahns work in the retail or **wholesale** trades. The government and military employ about 15 percent of the population. Since the 1990s, the computer industry has grown in Utah, providing thousands of jobs.

Utah has a growing software industry. Many companies are moving their computer chip manufacturing plants to Utah.

QUICK FACTS

McDonnell-Douglas, one of the nation's two largest airplane manufacturers, began building airplane parts in Utah in 1987.

Processing Utah's agricultural goods is an important industry. Flour mills and dairy and meat-packing plants operate near farming districts.

About 70 percent of the land in Utah is owned by either the federal or the state government.

The Bonneville Salt Flats, once the bed of an ancient lake, is now the site of high-speed automobile racing.

GOODS AND SERVICES

Utah has a **diverse** economy. Mining, farming, manufacturing, and tourism are the state's main economic activities. Utah's agricultural industry provides many important goods. Hay is often grown to feed livestock. Wheat is grown in the northern regions of the state. Vegetables and fruit, such as potatoes, pears, peaches, apples, and onions, are grown on irrigated farmland in the state. Greenhouse and nursery products are also produced in Utah.

About three-quarters of Utah's farm income is obtained from the sale of livestock and livestock products, such as beef, wool, lamb, and dairy products. **Poultry** products, especially turkeys and eggs, are also valuable goods in the state.

Utah is one of the nation's leading sheep-raising states. There are more than 500,000 sheep in Utah.

QUICK FACTS

WordPerfect, a popular word-processing computer program, was created by Alan Ashton and Bruce Bastian of Brigham Young University. This program was originally produced in Orem, Utah. Nine years after WordPerfect was launched, it had annual sales of $100 million.

Utah produces more mink **pelts** than any other state.

Salt Lake City is the state's major center for finance and trade, with many company head offices located there.

The most valuable products manufactured in Utah are computers and electronics.

Many different products are manufactured in the state, including computers and office equipment. Transportation equipment, which ranges from space vehicles to automobile parts are also manufactured in the state. Other products made in Utah include medical tools, blast furnaces, fabricated metals, and paper products.

The chemical industry, which manufactures medicines, is very important to the state. Food processing follows closely behind the chemical industry. Flour mills, dairy plants, and meat-packing plants are found near most major farming districts in Utah.

With so many goods produced in the state, there is need for an adequate supply of electricity. About 97 percent of Utah's electricity is generated by steam-driven power plants, which are fueled by low-sulphur coal. There is an increased growth of coal production in the Colorado Plateau, which has helped fuel the state's mining revenues. Utah also obtains some of its power from hydroelectric, or water-generated, plants.

There are about 13,000 farms in Utah, and the main crops grown are wheat, barley, and hay.

Each of the four posts in a hogan, the Navajo's sacred home, represented one of the four mountains in their homeland.

FIRST NATIONS

The first peoples to live in the area that is now Utah were **Paleo-Indians.** They inhabited the region about 10,000 to 12,000 years ago. These ancient peoples hunted large animals for food. Later, as the Paleo-Indians learned how to make better hunting weapons, they began to stay in one area rather than follow the animals they hunted. They lived in caves and shelters made from wood and rocks, and they gathered plants and berries for food.

About 2,000 years ago, two different groups of Native Peoples, the Anasazi and the Fremont, lived in the Utah area. The Anasazi lived in southern Utah. They grew corn, squash, and beans, and raised turkeys. The Anasazi lived in rock dwellings built into cliffs and canyons. They are known for the art they carved into, and painted on, the cliffs. The Fremonts lived in northern Utah and were hunter-gatherers.

By the 1300s, Utah was home to several major groups of Native Peoples: the Ute, Paiute, Shoshone, Gosiute, and the Navajo. The largest group was the Ute, who occupied eastern Utah. They lived in tepees and hunted bison.

Paiute wickiups were small, round huts covered with tule rushes.

Don Bernard Miera y Pacheco drew the first map of Utah. Pacheco was part of the Dominguez-Escalante expedition.

QUICK FACTS

In the early 1800s, beaver pelts were worth about $10, which was a grand sum at that time.

Jedediah Smith was the first man of European descent to cross Utah from north to south and then from west to east.

Jim Bridger is thought to have been the first man of European descent to reach the Great Salt Lake in 1824. He drank the lake water, but it was so salty that he immediately spat it out. He assumed that he had reached the Pacific Ocean.

Jim Bridger

EXPLORERS AND MISSIONARIES

The first European to travel to Utah was a Spanish explorer. Juan Maria Antonio de Rivera made it to the Colorado River, near present-day Moab, in 1765. In 1776, a group of explorers led by two Franciscan priests, Francisco Atanasio Dominguez and Silvestre Velez de Escalante, entered Utah. The Dominguez-Escalante **expedition** was searching for a route from New Mexico to California. The expedition was not very successful, and the group returned to Santa Fe. Over the next few decades, merchants from Sante Fe traded goods with the Native Peoples in Utah.

In the early 1800s, mountain men explored the region looking for beavers. They trapped the beavers, skinned them, and dried their pelts. In the spring, the trappers met for an annual gathering, called a rendezvous. At the rendezvous, trappers traded pelts with Native Peoples and company agents, and bought supplies. They also celebrated the year's success with eating, singing, and contests.

Utah has an annual festival celebrating the mountain men of the 1800s and their traditional annual rendezvous.

John Charles Frémont led three expeditions into the Oregon territory between 1842 and 1845.

EARLY SETTLERS

The United States government sent people to explore and settle the Utah area. In 1843, John Charles Frémont, a government explorer, visited the Great Salt Lake area. He returned to the region in 1845. John Charles Frémont mapped trails in Utah and described the plant and animal life he encountered in the Great Basin.

In 1846, the Donner-Reed expedition traveled by wagon train through Utah on its way to the West Coast. The terrain in Utah was challenging; the group had to clear a trail through the rough Wasatch Mountains and then cross an 80-mile salt desert west of the Great Salt Lake. Many people froze to death or starved. Only forty-four of the original eighty-seven people in the expedition survived.

QUICK FACTS

In the 1840s, when the beaver trade was declining, mountain men came to the Utah region less often.

Jedediah Smith was the first United States resident to reach California by land. He traveled from the Great Salt Lake to California and back in 1826 and 1827.

Early settlers to Utah, most of which were Mormon, applied for statehood about six times between 1849 and 1887. They finally entered the Union in 1896 as the forty-fifth state.

The Mormon Trail was pioneered by the Donner expedition.

Utah celebrates Pioneer Day on July 24—the day in 1848 that Brigham Young arrived in the state.

Brigham Young encouraged people to come to his settlement through the Perpetual Emigrating Fund. Newcomers could borrow money from the fund and pay it back after they were established.

In 1857, President James Buchanan, who believed that the Mormons were rebelling against the United States government, sent 2,500 soldiers into Utah to replace governor Brigham Young. This episode is referred to as the Utah War.

James Buchanan

Mormons were the first large group to settle in the Utah region. Led by Brigham Young, many Mormons left Nauvoo, Illinois, after their founder Joseph Smith was murdered. They made the 1,000-mile journey to the Great Salt Lake region in 1847 to escape religious **persecution**. The first group of Mormons, including 143 men, 3 women, and 2 children, reached the Great Salt Lake Valley on July 21, 1847.

Brigham Young, the second president of the Church of Jesus Christ of Latter-Day Saints, is credited with settling Utah.

The Mormons believed Utah was the place to create their own Zion, or kingdom of God. They began to plow and irrigate the land on the day they arrived. In 1848, their crops were threatened by a swarm of crickets. Fortunately, flocks of gulls flew to the region from the Great Salt Lake and ate many of the crickets.

The Mormons continued to work the land, building settlements. Spreading out, they created new settlements in neighboring areas. By 1860, about 40,000 Mormons had built more than 150 independent communities.

Since cooperation is an important part of the Mormon faith, early settlers farmed the land together with much success.

The population density in Utah is about twenty-six people per square mile.

QUICK FACTS

The population of Utah is 2,130,000.

Utah has one of the highest birth rates and lowest death rates in the country.

Only about 8.7 percent of Utahns are 65 years of age or more.

POPULATION

The majority of Utahns, about 90 percent, are of European descent. Other ethnic groups in the state include Asians and Pacific Islanders, Native Americans, Hispanic Americans, and African Americans. About 97 percent of Utahns were born in the United States. The rest were mostly born in Canada, Germany, or Mexico.

About 87 percent of Utah's residents live in urban areas. Highly populated cities include Salt Lake City, Provo, West Valley City, Sandy, and Orem.

Utah has an excellent education system. The state has the highest **literacy** rate in the United States. Also, about 90 percent of all Utahns graduate high school.

Utah has a very young population, with about 33 percent of its citizens under the age of eighteen. The national average for people under the age of eighteen is 13 percent, far less than Utah's average.

With about 174,400 people, Salt Lake City is the most populated city in the state.

The Capitol in Salt Lake City stands 165 feet tall at its highest point.

POLITICS AND GOVERNMENT

The Utah state government is divided into three branches. The governor is the head of the executive branch, which also includes the lieutenant governor, treasurer, auditor, and attorney general. Each of these officials is elected to four-year terms. The executive branch has more than fifty agencies that run state affairs.

The legislative branch, which creates state laws, includes the Senate and the House of Representatives. Twenty-nine senators serve two-year terms, while seventy-five representatives serve four-year terms. The judicial branch of government includes the Supreme Court and seven district courts.

QUICK FACTS

Utah is governed under a **constitution** that was adopted at the time of statehood in 1896.

Utah has two United States senators and three members in the nation's House of Representatives. The state has five presidential electoral votes.

The members of the Utah Supreme Court serve ten-year terms.

The Utah government's largest source of funds comes from federal grants and the state sales tax.

Utah was the fourth state in the nation to grant women the right to vote.

Regular meetings of the legislature begin on the second Monday in January. Sessions are limited to forty-five days a year.

Each member of the Utah House of Representatives is responsible for representing more than 22,000 people.

Construction of the Salt Lake Temple began six years after Brigham Young first came to Utah. It took forty years to complete.

CULTURAL GROUPS

Nearly 70 percent of all Utahns are Mormon, which means that they are members of The Church of Jesus Christ of Latter-day Saints. There are nearly 9 million practicing Mormons throughout the world. The headquarters for The Church of Jesus Christ of Latter-day Saints is located in Salt Lake City.

The Mormon religion places great importance upon community and family life. The church community is known to help and support members through difficult times. Mormons strive to dress modestly, and to avoid potentially harmful substances, such as alcohol. Team sports and other athletic activities are popular with Mormons, who believe in keeping their bodies strong and healthy. The Mormon community also values education and hard work.

QUICK FACTS

Smoking and drinking alcohol, coffee, or tea are prohibited by the Mormon religion. In fact, it is illegal to smoke in most public places in Utah.

On average, Utahns have a longer life span than people from other states. The rate of cancer in Utah is half the national average.

Most members of the Mormon Church have the opportunity to participate in the community by teaching classes and giving sermons.

Utah's Navajo are well known for their rug weaving.

Five main groups of Native Peoples live in Utah: the Ute, Navajo, Paiute, Goshute, and the Shoshone. There are about 3,300 Ute in the state. They have their own tribal government and control about 1.3 million acres of land. There are about 7,000 Utah Dine, also called Navajo, 700 Paiute, and more than 500 Goshute. Fewer than 400 Shoshone live in Utah.

Many Native Americans in Utah are working to create a Circle of Wellness Center. In Native-American culture, the circle represents the cycles of life. This center is designed to serve all Native Americans in the state, with a focus on education, community, culture, and economic development.

QUICK FACTS

The Dine believed that they traveled through four different worlds to get to the Four Corners area.

Utah has one of the lowest divorce rates in the nation.

UTAH DIVISION OF INDIAN AFFAIRS

UTAH COUNTIES & INDIAN RESERVATIONS

IDAHO

Northwestern Band Of Shoshoni

CACHE
BOX ELDER
RICH
WEBER
MORGAN
DAVIS
SUMMIT
DAGGETT
SALT LAKE
DUCHESNE
Uintah & Ouray Reservation (The Ute Tribe)
WASATCH
TOOELE
UINTAH
Skull Valley Goshute Tribe
UTAH
Goshute Tribe
JUAB
CARBON
SANPETE
MILLARD
Paiute Tribe Kanosh Band
EMERY
GRAND
SEVIER
Paiute Tribe Koosharem Band
Paiute Tribe Indian Peaks Band
BEAVER
PIUTE
WAYNE
IRON
Paiute Tribal Land (Cedar City)
GARFIELD
SAN JUAN
White Mesa Ute
WASHINGTON
Paiute Tribe (Shivwits Band)
KANE

WYOMING
NEVADA
COLORADO

ARIZONA
San Juan Southern Paiute (No reservation land)
Navajo Nation

ARTS AND ENTERTAINMENT

A variety of musicians have delighted audiences across the nation. The Mormon Tabernacle Choir is a world-famous choir that began in the late-1800s. Today, it has more than 300 singers and makes recordings as well as television and radio broadcasts. Choir members are chosen for their talent and their character. Some choir members are very dedicated, traveling long distances for rehearsals, broadcasts, and other events.

The Osmonds are a well-known family from Utah. Some of the brothers began singing together at a very early age, calling themselves the Osmond Brothers. In the 1960s, the Osmond Brothers performed on a variety of popular television shows. One of the brothers, Donny Osmond, began a solo career and became a teen idol. Donny Osmond had thirteen top forty records. Donny and his sister, Marie, had their own prime-time variety show from 1976 to 1979, and their own talk show in the late 1990s.

The Mormon Tabernacle Choir sang for the first time in 1847. Today, they perform all over the world.

QUICK FACTS

Donny Osmond's first number one single was "Go Away Little Girl."

Actors Roseanne Barr, Maude Adams, James Woods, and Loretta Young were all born in Utah.

Roseanne Barr

The Utah Symphony in Salt Lake City was founded in 1940. The symphony performs in Abravanel Hall, which is one of the largest symphony orchestra concert halls in the United States.

The Osmonds disbanded in 1980, after almost twenty years of success in the music business.

The Festival of the American West celebrates Western heritage, showcasing actors and entertainers dressed in historic clothing.

Various festivals are celebrated each year throughout Utah. The Utah Shakespeare Festival, founded in 1961, is held annually in Cedar City. As well as staging three Shakespearean plays every year, the festival has free "Green Shows" before each evening performance. Green Shows feature puppet shows, strolling vendors, musicians, and dancers.

The Festival of the American West is held in Wellsville during the last weekend of July. The fair gives visitors a taste of the Old West, with arts and crafts displays, a cowboy poetry contest, and outdoor performances with more than 200 entertainers. People can even witness a re-creation of a rendezvous, with participants dressed up as mountain men.

The Utah Shakespeare Festival received a Tony Award for outstanding regional theater.

QUICK FACTS

Many popular television shows have been produced in Utah, including *Touched by an Angel.*

People can explore the deep gorge at Grand Gulch Primitive Area, which has many Anasazi relics.

The area around Kanab is known as "Utah's Little Hollywood" because so many movies have been filmed there.

Some movies filmed in Utah include: *Indiana Jones and the Last Crusade* (1989), *Thelma and Louise* (1991), *Forrest Gump* (1994), and *The Wild Wild West* (1999).

Indiana Jones and the Last Crusade

SPORTS

Karl Malone is nicknamed "The Mailman" because he always delivers on the court.

QUICK FACTS

Utah has more than 1,000 fishable lakes and numerous fishing streams. Some of the fish found in Utah waters include rainbow trout, cutthroat, mackinaw, bass, walleye, and bluegill.

The region around Moab, especially Slickrock Trail, is a popular destination for mountain bikers.

At the 2002 Olympic Winter Games, the Winter Sports Park hosts bobsleigh, luge, and ski jumping.

Utah has fourteen downhill ski resorts. By automobile, seven of these ski resorts are less than an hour's drive from Salt Lake City.

Sports fans have many teams to cheer for in Utah. The state is home to several professional sports teams. The New Orleans Jazz, which began playing in 1974, moved to Salt Lake City to become the Utah Jazz. The Utah Jazz are members of the National Basketball Association. Players such as Karl "The Mailman" Malone and John Stockton have helped make the team popular throughout the state. Utah also has a team in the Women's National Basketball League, the Utah Starzz. The Utah Grizzlies are members of the International Hockey League. They are a "farm team," which is a team whose members can be drafted into the National Hockey League. The Utah Grizzlies also stand in for absent players of the National Hockey League's Dallas Stars.

The Utah Jazz have been at or above a 0.6 winning percentage for thirteen seasons.

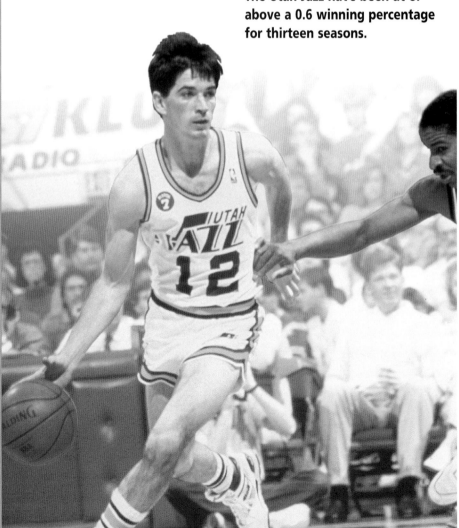

Utah's varied landscape and many bicycle trails are a biker's dream.

Utah's national parks and forests, as well as its mountain ranges, lakes, and rivers, are ideal for many types of recreational activities. Popular outdoor activities in Utah include camping, hunting, fishing, hiking, and horseback riding. Skiing and other winter sports are also enjoyed in the state. Utah has many ski resorts, including Powder Mountain, Sundance, Alta, and the Snowbird Ski and Summer Resort.

In 1995, Salt Lake City won the bid to host the 2002 Olympic Winter Games, held from February 8 to 24. Top athletes from around the world will compete in a variety of winter sports, including ski jumping, snowboarding, bobsleigh, luge, figure skating, and curling.

Children in Utah can take part in the Olympic experience through Youth Sport Programs. These programs allow children to participate in and learn about an Olympic sport. Seven different Youth Sport Programs are designed to fit any skill level. Students can take part in mock-Olympics at their schools. They can also learn a new sport at an official Olympic Winter Games location.

For adventurous Utahns, boating and river rafting are popular activities.

Brain Teasers

1 The first department store in the western United States opened up in Utah in 1868. Which store was it?

a) JCPenney

b) Target

c) Zions Co-operative Mercantile Institution (ZCMI)

Answer: c

2 When was the first transcontinental railroad in the nation completed?

a) 1803

b) 1850

c) 1869

d) 1899

Answer: c. It was completed in May 1869.

3 Place the following Utah cities in order from highest to lowest population: Orem, Salt Lake City, Provo, West Valley City, and Sandy.

Answer: Salt Lake City, Provo, West Valley City, Sandy, and Orem

4 Which one of the following people was not born in Utah?

a) Philo Farnsworth

b) Roseanne Barr

c) Jimmy Osmond

d) Brigham Young

Answer: d. Brigham Young was born in Vermont.

5

Who was the partner of the legendary outlaw, Butch Cassidy?

a) Robert Parker

b) Sundance Kid

c) Tonto

d) Miles Goodyear

Answer: b

6

What was the name for the annual gathering of mountain men?

a) Rendezvous

b) S'il vous plaît

c) Deseret

d) Pauite

Answer: a

7

How did sea gulls help early settlers in Utah?

Answer:
Sea gulls from the Great Salt Lake ate swarms of crickets that were destroying crops.

8

Where is the largest open-pit mine in the world?

Answer: Utah's Kennecott Copper Mine is the largest open-pit mine in the world. About 5.3 billion tons of material have been mined there since the mid-1800's. It is 2 miles across and 0.5 miles deep.

FOR MORE INFORMATION

Books

Bock, Judy and Rachel Kranz. *Scholastic Encyclopedia of the United States*. New York: Scholastic, 1997.

Fradin, Dennis B. *Utah (From Sea to Shining Sea)*. Chicago, IL: Children's Press, 1993.

Hicks, Roger. *The Big Book of America*. Philadelphia: Courage Books, 1994.

Web sites

You can also go online and have a look at the following Web sites:

The State of Utah
http://www.state.ut.us

Utah Travel Council
http://www.utah.com

50 States: Utah
http://www.50states.com/utah.htm

Some Web sites stay current longer than others. To find other Utah Web sites, enter search terms, such as "Utah," "Salt Lake City," "Great Salt Lake," or any other topic you want to research.

GLOSSARY

allosaurs: meat-eating dinosaurs of the late Jurassic period

annuals: plants that live through only one growing season

birds of prey: birds, such as eagles and hawks, that catch and eat other animals

burrow: a hole dug in the ground in which an animal or animals live

commemorate: to serve as a reminder

constitution: the document containing the laws by which a government must work

diverse: made up of many different elements

endangered: a threatened species

expedition: an journey made for exploration

fossil: a rock that contains evidence of an ancient organism, such as a leaf or bone print

irrigation: the supply of water to dry land using pipes, ditches, or streams

literacy: the ability to read and write

mountain range: a series of connected mountains that are similar in form

Paleo-Indian: a prehistoric human culture in the Western Hemisphere, believed to have migrated from Asia

paleontologist: a person who studies prehistoric life by examining early remains and fossils

pelt: the skin or hide of an animal with the fur still attached

persecution: unfair and cruel treatment of a person or people, usually based on religion, race, or beliefs

petroglyphs: prehistoric drawings or carvings on rock

poultry: fowl, such as chickens, turkeys, ducks, and geese, especially those valued for their meat and eggs

precipitation: moisture that falls to Earth's surface, such as rain, snow, or hail

stegosaur: a plant-eating dinosaur with a double row of upright bony plates along the back, long hind legs, a short neck, and a small head

transcontinental: extending across a continent

wholesale: the sale of a large quantity of goods, especially to retail stores

INDEX